Illustrations by Juls
j.wels@yahoo.com

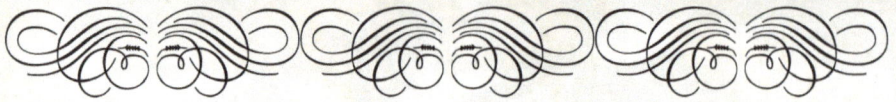

Table of Contents

Introduction

My interest in the Trust energy started in the fall of 2009. A friend of mine had been involved in some deep spiritual work and he said one of the fundamental keys was to have 100% Trust in God. At this time I was not able to participate in the type of program he had been involved in, but I did not want to wait. I decided to begin my own program of trusting God 100%.

What I did was to sit in my chair and ask to be filled with Trust energy. My idea was if I was filled with Trust energy then it would open me up to trusting God. In my meditations I began to be filled with an energy that I knew as Trust. At times I felt that I might burst because there was so much energy happening inside of me. I have related this practice to you with the 'Connecting to Trust Exercise.'

What I noticed is that no matter where I was at when I started the exercise when I became filled with the Trust energy I was in more of a flow with myself and my life; everything seemed to move smoother. I felt better about myself. I had more self-worth and confidence. I felt more open and connected to other people. What was even more significant to me is that my life started to function in a more positive and successful way. It seemed that as long as I was filled with the Trust energy then everything would work out. When I felt low on Trust energy then I would take a moment to reconnect to the Trust energy and fill my tanks up again.

These positive benefits kept increasing as I did this exercise more and more. I began to share this exercise with other people and they were having similar results as I was, so I knew I was onto something. I tried to research what people had taught about trust, but I could not find any information. Everything I came up with was on my own. Later on I did find some teachings that corroborated

1

what I had realized. I was glad I had these realizations before I found the other information because this way I knew I had really experienced it and I had not skewed my perception to fit someone else's idea.

The acid test came in the spring of 2010. One day I was walking my dog when I started having a great deal of pain in the upper part of my throat where the tonsils are located. It got so bad I had to lay down in the fetal position until the pain passed. This took 5 to 10 minutes. The day before this happened I had a conversation with some friends about their daughter who was allergic to nuts. I get hay fever in the spring and because of my conversation with my friends I thought I must be having a severe allergic reaction to something; maybe even anaphylactic shock as my friend's daughter had. My breathing was not affected. I could still take deep breaths with no constriction in my chest. I did not have chest pains or change in my heart pulse or strength. There was no dizziness, nausea or pain down my left arm. This onset of pain happened a few more times over the next few weeks. I had traveler's insurance where you pay out of pocket and then get reimbursed. I had just come back from a trip, so I did not have the money to go to a doctor. After a few more incidences I decided if it ever happened again that I would get some money and go to a doctor no matter what.

In June, 2010, I was staffing a seminar in Holland. After dinner I walked up some stairs and my heart started pounding so hard it felt like it would burst out of my chest. I made it to the top of the stairs and went into a room where two friends were talking. I lay on the bed and told them something weird was going on. One was a nurse so I felt somewhat safe. After the incident passed I realized I needed to take some action. We were in the countryside far away from everything, but a friend was coming that night and I would leave with him in the morning to see a doctor.

2

The next day I went back to Utrecht, the city I lived in, and saw a doctor who worked next to Diakonessenhuis hospital. The doctor said she would put me into the hospital and I asked her why. She said because I had an increased heart rate with severe pains and this is an automatic decision. I said the pain was all in my throat. She told me that when you have heart problems the pain can show up anywhere from the lower back to the shoulders, anywhere. I was only 200 meters from the entrance of the hospital, but she wanted me to take an ambulance. I thought this was crazy and I did not want to pay $3,000 for a 200 meter ride, so I walked instead.

On the way there I started to feel some pain and realized the doctor had made the right decision to admit me to the hospital. I got to the cardiac ward and was set up in an intensive care room for observation. As strange as it may seem this began what I consider two of the best weeks of my life.

On Monday I had an angiogram procedure. During this procedure I started having another severe angina attack that lasted at least 8 minutes. I was in severe pain and tears, not only that, but the doctor performing the procedure said he was 90% sure that I would need a triple bypass as I had three arteries that were 99% blocked. I also had another blockage of 70% on one of the arteries.

Until this point all of the angina attacks happened after I ate or when I was physically exerting myself. That changed the day after the angiogram. At 4:00 PM I was laying in bed and I had the most severe attack to date. Whenever I had an attack the nurses would ask me on a scale of 1 to 10 how severe the attack was; with 10 being the most painful thing I had ever felt. This attack on Tuesday went straight to 10 and then beyond .... and then beyond again. I called it a 12.

3

While it was happening I was sure I was not going to make it through. My heart was beating so hard it felt as if it would break my ribs. Each time it beat I thought my heart would split in two or shred into 100 pieces. I was being as still and calm as possible because I felt any effort to stop this attack from happening would only create some resistance that my heart would then have to work even harder to overcome. While this was happening I thought I should pray to live and then I heard a voice inside say something that I can still hear to this day and which is the basis of this book. It said, "Don't bother yourself with that. Just make sure that you keep feeling 100% Trust energy so whatever the next step is in your soul's evolution will be made in complete Trust." I thought, "Wow...Oh, my God!' and then just watched to see if I would live or not. Well, obviously I made it through, but I was very blown away, to say the least.

At this point I feel I should bring in some other factors to what was happening. Technically I did not have heart attacks. If there is no damage to the heart, if no cells die, then it is considered angina and not a heart attack. However, there was a man in my cardiac rehabilitation class that taught at the University of Utrecht. On his way home one day he felt some chest pain and rode his bike to the hospital instead of going home. He had heart damage. There were 3 times I had to stop riding a bike and lay down on the side of the road until the pain passed. I rated those times a '7'. I had 12 occurrences of '7' and above, plus over a dozen attacks that were less than a '7'. I did not have heart damage, so technically I did not have a heart attack, but I had 12 angina attacks more severe than the man who rode his bike to the hospital and had heart damage. I had clogged arteries and a strong heart, or as I like to say, 'I had a car with a good engine, but 3 flat tires', that is why I made it through the

4

attacks. My father was rated in the top 10 marathoners in the 60 and over age group for the USA. I got lucky and inherited his strong heart.

The reason I am saying this is because when I had these severe attacks my heart was automatically thrown into survival mode. It flooded my body with the most intense fear I have ever felt in my life. Now, most people would say fear is the opposite of trust. However, that was not my experience. Even though I was flooded with the most intense fear I have ever felt, I was naturally situated 100% in the Trust energy. Letting go to the fear actually blew my energy wide open and when everything would settle down I would always feel tremendous peace and Love. When everything opened up inside of me during the attack on Tuesday I had the experience of being immersed in a fountain of Trust and what was coming out of it was pure Light and Love. This is why I said it was two of the most wonderful weeks of my life because I kept having these attacks and kept getting opened up to more and more and more Light and Love.

The next morning, a Wednesday, I was writing a letter to a friend. While I was writing this letter one of the nurses came by and told me that the council of cardiac doctors had decided to implant stents instead of performing a triple bypass. I was soooooo relieved. I wrote to my friend a statement that is one of the basic tenets of what I feel living in the Trust energy is all about. 'When I live in the trust energy my life seems to be a procession of one prayer after another being answered, even when I do not consciously know what the prayer being answered is.'

Four days later on Saturday I had an even stronger attack than on Tuesday. I rated it a 14. The same phenomenon happened where I got completely blown wide open and was feeling so much Trust, Light and Love. During

5

this week I actually had some slight regrets that once I got stents to open the blockages and be released from the hospital that I would miss the opening created from all the fear. Of course, I am glad I got proper medical care, but it does speak to what a powerful experience all the fear and Trust were creating.

This experience in the hospital verified to me what I had been discovering and realizing about the Trust energy. The most important point being that no matter what is happening you can consciously live 100% in the Trust energy.

Part One

The Energy
Of
TRUST WORKS !

TRUST is an energy that enters your being through the heart. Trust is not something you need to work at or have a break-through to get to. It is unconditional and available to anyone in unlimited amounts if they would just become aware of it.

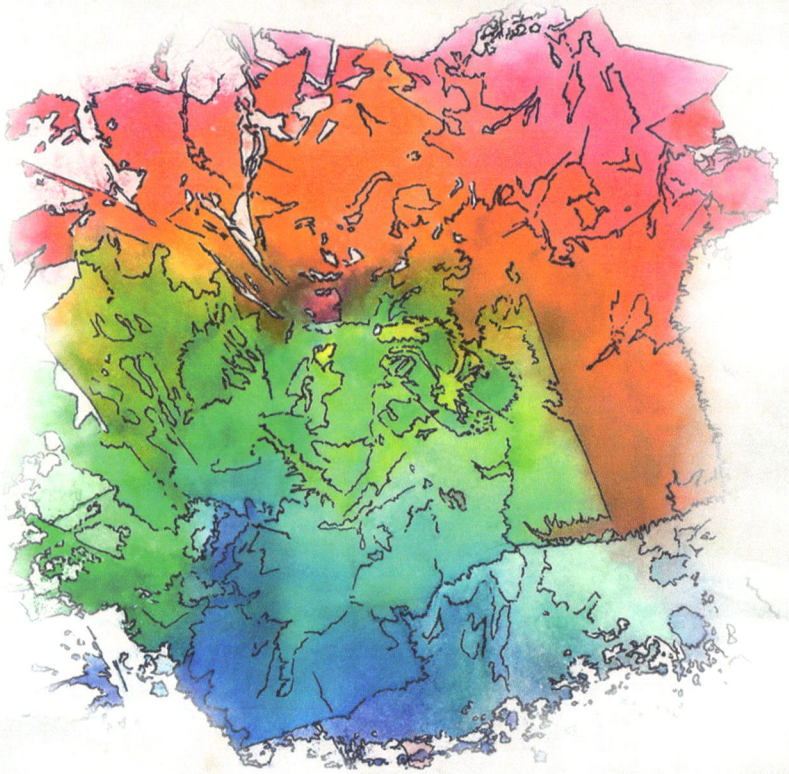

Trust is a Divine energy ! ! !
The Trust energy is one of God's gifts to mankind.
It is an energy that enables us to live in this world and keep
contact with the Divine at the same time. This is what the
logo on the cover represents. When we need to go to the
depth where we are in connection to the Divine then we can
use the Trust energy to go deeply inside. This going inside is
depicted by the openness in the center of the heart.
When we need something in our material life we visualize
our desire and put our trust energy into it so our desire
will manifest.
This ability to manifest is depicted with the feeling of
taking what is in your heart and bringing it out into the
world.

The heart has two functions;
It pumps blood and moves the energy of Trust.
This is why the Trust energy is available to you in
unlimited supplies all of the time.

Trust is the flow ! ! !

It is not important what you do with TRUST nearly as much as it is important that you feel the energy of TRUST that is flowing through you at all times.

'When I live in the trust energy my life seems to be a procession of one prayer after another being answered, even when I do not consciously know what the prayer being answered is.'

Trust Works

Trust energy is the fuel and lubricant that keeps the Wheel of Life turning. The more I feel the Trust energy, then the more things flow. When I had the experience in the hospital of a fountain of Trust energy providing the foundation for unlimited flow of Light, Love and Truth it verified that idea even more. Think for yourself how many times you were moving along in some area of life or with some feeling and then things stopped. How many times have you heard yourself or someone else say, 'I do not trust.' Or 'I do not have enough trust?' Tapping back into the Trust energy will get things moving again. It may not solve all of your problems, but it keeps your mind and heart open, which enables you to receive solutions to your questions while at the same time providing the energy to put those solutions into motion and move forward in a positive manner. This is why I say Trust is the fuel and lubricant to keep the Wheel of Life turning.

Since the Trust energy helps you keep your heart
open. Trust is a basis for unconditional Love.

I call the place in my heart that the Trust energy flows through 'The Place of Trust'. In the Place of Trust the Trust energy brings about our good qualities. At the same time it pushes away uncertainty and doubt, frees you from suffering and brings you into a state of peace and happiness. In the Place of Trust I experience an alive calmness. It is not because I have unhooked myself from worries and anxieties, but more that worries and anxiety do not even exist in the Place of Trust.

Instead of having a defined sense of ego, the sense of self is a flow of the qualities known as the Fruits of the Holy Spirit (see page 36). Reality is more a feeling of unlimited, positive possibilities for success, rather than living in negativity and trying to prevent failure.

I came to this realization when I had repeated experiences of being caught up in negativity and having a difficult time getting out of it. Then I simply decided to feel Trust energy and the negativity automatically disappeared. After this happened numerous times I realized that in The Place of Trust negativity does not exist.

I have a friend that also had the same experience after practicing the Connecting to Trust Exercise. He told me that he used to practice calming exercises and he could center himself and find calm in the middle of the worries, but they were still circling around him. When he practiced feeling the Trust energy the worries were not even there. He has OCD, obsessive-compulsive disorder, so if it works for him in this way then this is very strong evidence that this exercise works.

16

The Place of Trust

The more you open to the Trust energy
and become situated in the Place of Trust,
the more you will be living and directing your life
with awareness from your heart,
instead of thinking from your brain.
That in itself nurtures a step forward
in the quality of your life
and the experience of who you truly are.

Feeling the Trust energy in the Place of Trust
Makes it easier to stay present in the moment.
Mainly because there are less disturbances
And distractions to pull on your awareness

The reality you will experience when living in the Place of Trust is going to seem new and different to what you are used to. However, upon examination you will find it feels more real, more open, much more positive and just makes more sense than the reality people have been conditioned and accustomed to accepting as true and real.

Accept it.

Live in it.

Rejoice in it.

There is something about the Trust energy that pushes away confusion and clears up the mind.

It opens our minds to new areas and to new avenues of thinking.

Trust is an energy that enables us to live in the expansive openness that exists in the realm of positive possibility and success, instead of the constrictive state of worry, dread and fear of failure.

This enables us to be open to all kinds of answers that never would have occurred to us or did not even have a chance of being recognized with our normal ways of thinking and regular point of view we are accustomed to using.

If you have trust you can always climb for more and reach higher and higher levels and it makes the spiritual path easier.

Living in the Place of Trust will not ensure that your life will be smooth and easy. You will still have obstacles and challenges ahead of you. What living in the Place of Trust will do is make it easier to face and go through those obstacles and challenges than if you were not living your life in the Place of Trust.

The more you approach the obstacles and challenges in your life with Trust the more you will see this is true. This will build up an energy of encouragement to keep living in the Place of Trust. You have to face these obstacles anyway, so why not do it with a powerful tool that will make it as smooth as possible?

Trust keeps pride down and is the root of devotion. There is something about trust that does not lead to developing more pride and ego.

When people get more energy and vitality they often think they are better than others because they are stronger and healthier than other people.

When people get more knowledge or wisdom they often think they are better than others because they are smarter than other people.

When people open up their feelings they often think they are better than others because they feel more than other people.

I cannot tell you why, but Trust does not bring about this feeling of being better than others. I can only say that the nature of trust is not about good or bad, right or wrong, better or less. In the Place of Trust there is more of a feeling of equality and connection.

The proof of this is how many times have you heard someone boast that they had so much trust? It just is not something people boast about.

From your experience of tapping into the Trust energy you may come to the realization that it is always available in unlimited supplies 24 hours a day, 7 days a week. This realization of trust being unlimited can change your perception of reality and how you go about living your life. Most people think of trust as a limited commodity and that the most important aspect of trust is what you do with it. They think they could lose it, break it, misuse it, abuse it or it could get damaged in some way. They also think it is only available to them if they make a great effort or have some good fortune.

Let us use an analogy of money. Imagine you received one billion US dollars every day. Would you be concerned if you made an investment and lost money, or loaned money to someone that did not pay it back? You probably would not become overly concerned because you most likely would have money from previous days, or at the very least you would be getting one billion US dollars tomorrow and then again the next day. Imagine how much less stress and anxiety you would have just from this one realization about the unlimited nature of the trust energy.

Also, I am not suggesting that you need to do anything with the trust energy. You may just want to sit in the satisfaction and fulfillment of experiencing it. What I am suggesting is it is more critical that you just feel the trust energy and trust in that rather than do anything special with it.

Unlimited amounts of unconditional Trust Energy is
available all of the time under all circumstances.

Trust Vs. Resistance

I do not regard fear as the opposite of trust. In my experience resistance is the opposite of trust.

Trust makes things work.
Trust makes things move.
Fear can move.

In fact, when you let go into fear it often creates great movement. Think about all the feelings that happen during scary movies or roller coasters. There is often a lot of screaming and energy moving in those times.

Think of the aliveness of children and how they run around and scream.
Think of the excitement when you take a risk.
There are lots of feelings moving when you take a risk and take actions to move forward.
When I was in the hospital and having heart attacks I had tremendous fear flowing out of my heart. At the same time I felt the most trust I have ever experienced. It surprised me, but it was true.

It is resistance that stops movement.
It is resistance that slows things down and gets thing jammed up.
In fact, the thought I had during my heart attacks that were full of fear was, 'Don't fight it'.

That feeling of Trust energy is what the heart and soul truly desire. That is why I say 'TRUST IS DELICIOUS' because once you get a taste of it, then you will want more and more and more Trust energy AND the nice part of this is you can have as much Trust energy as you desire anytime you want it. My experience is that when we are not conscious of all the Trust energy happening in our life and we have Trust issues, then our heart and soul feel deprived of an energy they feel is essential in the same manner our lungs and heart would feel deprived of an essential energy if we did not breathe and were running low on oxygen. A great deal of time and energy is often spent in trying to amass control and power in our lives in order to have a feeling that we can exert some influence on how our lives will be. This type of behavior stems from a belief that we need things to be a certain way so we can be happy. Once you have the experience of the Trust energy then it will cut down on what you feel you need to do in your life in order to feel satisfaction and fulfillment because what the Trust energy opens you up to is soooooo very satisfying and fulfilling all by itself.

Sometimes people say they do not trust,
but everything we do is based on trusting
something.
So trust is always happening.
It is to your benefit to acknowledge and
feel the trust that is always flowing
through you.

'Trust vs. Beliefs'

People say that it is our beliefs that are responsible for what manifests in our life. My experience is where we place our Trust is what determines what manifests in our life. Since we most often place trust in certain beliefs, then it would only make sense that it would seem it is the beliefs that are the determining factor. However, once we take a slightly deeper look then we can see it is the trust that gives these beliefs the fuel and energy to manifest in the material world.

Anti-Trust Highway

Most people, practically everyone, relates to Trust as if it is a belief or attitude. Trust is an energy. The notion that Trust is something to get to, to find or to bring about by our effort is erroneous. We live in a state of trust 24/7. Why people do not experience this reality of trust is that they have been trained since they were born to place trust into their mind instead of feeling it in their hearts. Whether we are building up a version of ourselves that would be considered positive like a great artist, worker, athlete, etc., or we build up a negative image, it is all living under the influence of the ego instead of living in the Trust energy that is constantly happening in our hearts. I call this process of placing the energy of Trust into concepts, beliefs or judgments in the mind 'living on the Anti-Trust Highway'.

Living from our minds depletes so much of the positive potential the Trust energy has compared to when we live in the Trust energy in the Place of Trust. Don`t fight the fear.

Let the Trust energy flow.

I have written in a way that some people may interpret as you do not do anything but feel the trust energy and let life happen.

Well, wouldn't that be nice.

There are times to take action and times to sit back.

When taking action you may want to consider taking action in harmony with Ho' oponopono.

It is a Hawaiian practice of forgiveness. In my own experience I feel the source of Ho' oponopono and the Place of Trust are the same or at least exist at the same depth.

Ho' oponopono and living in the Trust energy go hand-in-hand.

Try it and see how it is for you.

Ho' oponopono

Ho' oponopono is a Huna practice of atonement,
reconciliation and forgiveness.
It is based on the truth that we are all one and
everything is interconnected.
Everyone is responsible for everything that happens.
Not only for yourself, but for others too.
If an earthquake, flood, tsunami or other natural
disaster strikes,
Then practice Ho' oponopono,
If someone meets some type of hardship,
Then practice Ho' oponopono,
If someone does something that hurts you,
Then practice Ho' oponopono.

The mantra to practice is:
I am sorry.
I love you.
Please forgive me.
Thank you.

Sink into the place where you feel connected to
your heart.
Sometimes I use it just to tap into the feeling of
Ho' oponopono.

IT WORKS!

Two Wolves

One evening an old Cherokee told his grandson about a battle that goes on inside people.

He said, "My son, the battle is between two wolves inside us all.

One is Evil. It is negative, anger, hate, envy, jealousy, sorrow, regretful, greed, selfish, self-pity, guilt, arrogant, resentful, inferiority, superiority, dishonest, and deceitful.

The other is Good. It is joy, peace, love, hope, serenity, humility, kindness, benevolence, empathy, generosity, truth, compassion and faith".

The grandson thought about it for a minute and then asked his grandfather: "Which wolf wins?"
The old Cherokee simply replied, "The one you feed."

The wolf you feed is the wolf you put your trust into.
The power to control the quality of your life is in your choice.
It is a moment-by-moment, situation-by-situation decision making process.

It is your choice.

Do you want to follow the way of the White Wolf and live in the Place of Trust and manifest the Fruits of the Holy Spirit?
OR
Do you want to follow the way of the Dark Wolf with all of its negativity?

The Way of the White Wolf

Fruits of the Holy Spirit

Joy

Love

Peace

Humility

Kindness

Goodness

Gentleness

Self-control

Faithfulness

The Way of the Dark Wolf

Negativity

Anger	Hate
Envy	Jealousy
Sorrow	Regret
Greed	Selfish
Self-pity	Guilt
Arrogance	Resentful
Superiority	Inferiority
Dishonest	Deceitful

Praying With The Trust Energy

The Trust energy has a benevolent, positive and innate intelligence that is designed to work for the highest good. Using the Trust energy when you pray is very effective. It is a very simple method. Think of the area you want something to happen in. Fill it with the Trust energy and then let if go. Then watch what happens.

TRUST

The path of living in the Trust energy is a simple and highly rewarding way of life. It is simple because doing the 'Connecting to the Trust Energy Exercise' is simple and the basis for walking the path of the Trust energy. It is highly rewarding because the Trust energy is always working. When the Trust energy becomes more centered in our hearts, then it naturally works for our highest good.

At any one point in time each of us has a certain amount of Trust energy is our system. This amount we have in our system is what I refer to as 'The Ball of Trust Energy'. This Ball of Trust energy will increase as we practice the 'Connecting to the Trust Energy Exercise' and continually fill ourselves with the Trust energy.

At first we start off with the vast majority of the
Trust energy concentrated in the brain and ego/mind.

As we practice 'The Connecting to the Trust Energy Exercise', then we start to dissolve and break down the Anti-Trust Highway. As the Anti-Trust Highway dissolves and breaks down, then the Ball of Trust Energy in our hearts increases and the amount of Trust Energy in our brains decreases.

Eventually the Ball of Trust Energy increases enough that it becomes our dominant energy and we are walking on the Path of Trust Energy.

Part Two

The Trust Exercises

Try the 'Connecting to Trust
Energy Exercise' for 10 days
and you will that what I say in
this book is true.
Practice the 'Connecting to Trust
Energy Exercise' for 40 days
and you may never want to stop.

CONNECTING TO TRUST ENERGY EXERCISE

The object of this meditation is to become filled with the feeling and energy of Trust; not Trust in one thing or another, but to just feel and experience the core energy of Trust that is constantly flowing through our being.

It is simple and I will explain it for you.
• Go inside and begin to feel what you would call 'Trust'. Sometimes it is helpful to think of a person, place or thing that you feel Trust in to use that as a beginning point. It could be the Trust you have placed in your friends, your work, your talents, your health, where you like to go for holidays, etc.

• Some of the signs of feeling Trust are:
  o A feeling of safety and security
  o Love and joy
  o A feeling of inner strength
  o Feeling the ability to move forward or to manifest your desires
  o Courage
  o A feeling and attitude of determination: as in 'Yes!
  o Openness and vulnerability, but with an positive sense of strength instead of the feeling of being susceptible to harm or getting hurt in some way

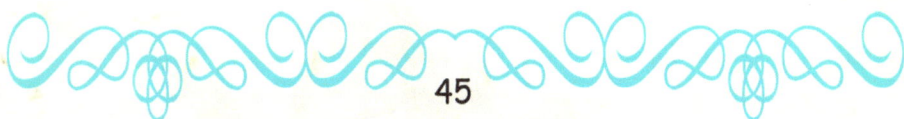

• After 5-10 minutes when the feeling and energy of Trust has grown and moved as much as it appears it is going to, then begin to separate the image of the person, place or thing you have used to inspire the feeling and energy of Trust from the feeling and energy. It is not necessary for the object to disappear completely, just that you can at least establish the difference between the person, place or thing and the feeling and energy of Trust. It is similar to when you love someone. That person is the object of your love and not the love you feel. Make a similar distinction with the Trust energy.

• Let this feeling of Trust energy grow in whatever way it naturally becomes for you. Each person's experience will be different in what they are experiencing, SO DO NOT JUDGE YOUR SELF OR OTHERS.

• You may not have the experience of the Trust changing in depth, size or strength. It may just stay as it is. If this happens, then do not fret or worry. Nothing is wrong. If you feel Trust you have succeeded.

• As you practice this exercise your experience of the Trust energy will continue to grow deeper and be more open and available for you. If and when it does grow it may even fill you completely from head to toe. If this happens then let it grow into something bigger once it has filled you. Maybe it can fill the room or your city or even the world

• That is the exercise. It is simply real and real simple.

This is an exercise to see how Trust produces a positive perception of life, or at least a more positive perception of things then when there is negativity and fear.

Exercise: If you have an area you are working on then revisit it and see how it looks when you have Trust in your focus and vision instead of fear.

I have found that answers and solutions happen easier and that things tend to work out to at least an acceptable degree when I am living in a state of Trust. At the very least I am not filled with the torment and suffering I experience when I am looking with fear, doubt or worry.

EVERYTHING YOU THINK IS TRUE IS WHAT YOU TRUST !!!

There is a way to find Trust in what you think you do not Trust.
You may think you do not Trust something.
BUT EVERYTHING YOU THINK IS TRUE IS WHAT YOU TRUST ! ! !
When asked why you do not Trust that 'something' then you will invariably say, "Well, BECAUSE......."

• Whatever comes after the word BECAUSE is what you Trust.
• Whatever comes after the word BECAUSE is what you believe to be true.
• If you remove the BECAUSE from your thinking then the energy that is left is Trust.
• If you are not able to remove all of the 'BECAUSE', but you can at least distinguish that there is an energy independent of the 'BECAUSE', then you have succeeded.

www.ingramcontent.com/pod-product-compliance
Lightning Source LLC
Chambersburg PA
CBHW041742040426
42443CB00004B/88